Hey, That's not fair!

M. Christine Stephens

Copyright @2022 by M. Christine Stephens

All rights reserved. No part of this book may be reproduced in any form or by any electronic or mechanical means, including information storage and retrieval systems, without permission in writing from the publisher, except by reviewers, who may quote brief passages in a review.

This publication contains the opinions and ideas of its author. It is intended to provide helpful and informative material on the subjects addressed in the publication. The author and publisher specifically disclaim all responsibility for any liability, loss or risk, personal or otherwise, which is incurred as a consequence, directly or indirectly, of the use and application of any of the contents of this book.

WORKBOOK PRESS LLC
187 E Warm Springs Rd,
Suite B285, Las Vegas, NV 89119, USA

Website: https://workbookpress.com/
Hotline: 1-888-818-4856
Email: admin@workbookpress.com

Ordering Information:
Quantity sales. Special discounts are available on quantity purchases by corporations, associations, and others.
For details, contact the publisher at the address above.

Library of Congress Control Number:
ISBN-13: 978-1-952754-26-5 (Paperback Version)
         978-1-952754-27-2 (Digital Version)

REV. DATE: 03/5/2022

Hey, That's not fair!

M. Christine Stephens

To my daughter, Jenell, and my son, Dustin. It is from their eyes I have tried to write it; it is into their world I try to reach with the precious truth of God's love.

1

Sometimes things aren't fair. I have to eat all my dinner, but my brother sneaks and gives his to our dog when my mom is not looking. He hardly even gets in trouble, but I did that one time and I got in trouble. Our dog even licks his plate, and Mom would freak about that if she knew. Sometimes, I tell on my brother. I get a little bit happy if he gets yelled at.

My brother never feeds my cat, then my father makes me do it, even when I tell him that it is not my turn. He says, "Just do it anyway because if you were a cat, you would want someone to feed you."

That's not fair. I have to do my brother's stuff, and I don't get paid any extra allowance for it. He still gets all of his allowance. I tried to tell this to my dad. He just said that no matter what other people do, I need to what's right.

Sometimes, I feel like I'm not as good as other kids, because sometimes they can run faster, or they are prettier, or they are smarter than me. Some kids are richer than me. Some kids seem like they get everything they want. I told Mom about that. She said that I am just as good as all those kids. She said God made me and He loves me and that just goes to show how good I am. She said that God gives everyone something special, and if I ask Him to show me the special thing He gave me, He will.

Some kids make fun of the way I look. It makes me mad, then it makes me cry. Dad said I'm not what other people say I am. I am Gods child. A special one whom He loves. Dad said it doesn't matter what other people think I am because God made me just how He wanted me. Dad said God loved me even before I was born. He loved me when I was still inside of Mom. He even knew who I was then. Isn't that cool?

Sometimes I think my mother and father like my sister better than they like me. I didn't tell that for a long time, then I did. They said they like us all the same, but sometimes I don't think so. It makes me feel like I almost hate my brothers and sisters. Sometimes, I don't know who else to tell that to, so I tell it to Jesus in my heart. In my heart, I hear Him say He loves me just as much as anyone else.

When everyone in the neighborhood laughs at Lindsey, I want to do it too. She is a little bit weird. She walks funny, with her foot crooked, and then her shoe gets all saggy on one side. Her sock gets all messed up. It looks dumb. Dad told me not to laugh at Lindsey. He tried to help me remember how it felt when people laughed at my freckles. How it made me mad and want to cry. He told me when you make fun of someone else, it hurts God, because God made that person. God loves Lindsey the same way that He loves me. I never thought about it that way before.

Amber next door has cool clothes. Her bicycle and her roller skates are better than mine. All her toys are new, and she still gets more new ones when it's not even her birthday. Even though she's my friend, sometimes that makes me not like her. I told Mom about that, and I thought Mom would get me new stuff too.

But Mom told me that even when I grow up, there are gonna be people who have neater stuff than I do. I still don't think it's fair. Mom also said that I have some neater stuff than other kinds have, and I should thank God for the neat things He gave me. I try to.

Sometimes, kids make fun of me because I have about a million freckles on my face. My sister doesn't have any. They call me "Red" and "Spot" and say I have pimples. I say I don't care, but it really makes me feel like crying. Sometimes in my room, when nobody is looking, I do cry.

But then I remember a place in my Kid's Bible where it says that God made everything about me and He loves me just the way I am. That helps me feel better, a little.

Tiffany in my class is smarter than me. She gets more stars on the board than I do, even if I try real hard to do my work right. Everybody else knows it too. I told Mom. Mom said maybe being so smart is Tiffany's gift from God. My dad told me to try not to be jealous of her, but instead to ask God what gift He gave me. Mom said if I asked God and then listened in my heart, He would answer me. So I tried it, and it worked. God told me that I have a gift too. It is laughter. I can make people laugh and I make them happy. That's why I have a lot of friends. I am not as smart as Tiffany, but she is not as cheerful and as much fun as I am.

Sometime, I don't like to sleep in my own bed. I know it's not really real but I think there is a monster or an alligator under my bed that will only get me in the middle of the night. I'm afraid to let my feet dangle over the edge. It makes me scared to death. But I remember a place in my Kid's Bible where it says that God will never leave me, and that He watches over me. I guess this means in the middle of the night too.

I think my dad forgot to help me comb my hair. My shirt's a little dirty, too.

My friend who lives next door to me only lives in our neighborhood on weekends. Her mom and dad got a divorce, and she always lives with her mother on school days, but she lives with her dad on weekends. Her T-shirts are never clean, and neither are her tennis shoes. Her hair is never combed. I told Mom that. Mom said maybe her dad isn't real careful about keeping her stuff clean. Maybe her dad has a hard time doing all that stuff by himself. Mom said I shouldn't think badly of other people because I might not understand everything about their life.

Shelly sits beside me on the school bus every morning on the way to school, but she does not sit beside me on the way home from school because her other friend Julie is there. After school, Shelly sits with Julie and I get left out. It seems like Shelly just likes me when her other friend is not around. That hurts my feelings a lot. I wanted to stop being her friend at all, but instead I think I'll talk to her about how I feel. I think a real friend will understand.

My friend lives two houses down from me. She took my scooter and didn't even ask me. When she brought it back, the back tire was flat. I am mad at her, and I don't even want to be her friend anymore. Dad fixed the tire with a patch. He said I have to forgive my friend. I don't think I should have to forgive her. She was wrong to take my scooter and break it. Dad even knows she is wrong.

But Dad said that we have to learn to forgive other people, even when it is hard. Dad said God forgives the bad things we do, and He tells us to forgive other people. I tried, but I can't do this by myself. Dad said I can tell God how hard it is, and He will help me do it.

My pastor at church said that we should tell other people about Jesus, and about how He died on the cross for all of us. Sometimes I want to, but I don't because I'm afraid my friends will think it's dumb, or that I'm too good and holy. But Jesus is so neat that I wish everyone knew about Him. I wish sometimes I wasn't too shy to tell people that Jesus died for our sins.

If I ask God, He will help me be brave enough to tell everyone. I don't want to worry about what people think of me, but sometimes I do. One time, I did tell my friend and she though Jesus was cool too, and she asked Jesus to come into her heart.

Sometimes I think other people are very bad. They do things, real bad things, worse than I would ever do. I might be a little bit bad sometimes, but I would never be as a bad as they are. My friend said good people go to heaven and bad people go to hell. But that is not really true. Even people who do bad things can go to heaven if they accept Jesus as their Savior.

Even good people can go to hell if they don't know that Jesus died on the cross for them. Mom said all people sin; good and bad people sin. Jesus came to die on the cross for all people. He paid the price for everyone's sins. Even mine. If Jesus hadn't died on the cross for my sins, I would have to go to hell, but Jesus loves me. He does not want me to go to hell. So He paid for my sins even though Jesus never sinned.

Last Saturday, all of my friends were throwing rocks at the birds in Jimmy's backyard. I knew I shouldn't do that, and I really didn't even want to do it that much, but I did it anyway because they were all doing it. I didn't want to be mean, but I just didn't want those guys to think I was a sissy. Anyway, everyone else is doing it too. Mr. Jacob told my dad I did that. My dad got mad. He told me no matter what other people do, I should always do what's right. Dad said if we all got in trouble for that, I would have to answer for the things I did, not my friends.

My friends were messing around with their jumping ropes after school. I have a cool neon yellow one. Everyone was trying to jump twenty-five jumps without missing one single jump. I wanted to try it, but I didn't because everyone was watching me, and I was afraid I would mess up. My brother told me to try it anyway, but I wouldn't. My brother said that if you never try things, you'll never get to do neat things. He said to try not to worry about messing up. He said even if you do mess up, it's okay 'cause you can always try again. He said lots of important people, who made neat things and did cool things, messed up sometime too, but they kept trying.

Amber and Lindsey are my friends. We are all friend together, but sometimes when Amber is not outside with us, Lindsey says mean things about her. One time, I said something mean about Amber too. I knew I shouldn't say mean things, but I did anyway. Then Lindsey told Amber that I said something mean about her, and she was sad and mad.

I really didn't mean to make Amber sad and mad. I wish I was never mean to her, because she really is my friend. My mom said I should tell Amber I am sorry and ask her to forgive me. Mom said she hoped I learned to never say mean things about anyone again. Jesus had lots of friends when He was here. He never said mean things about them. I'm going to try to act more like Jesus.

My room is always a stinky mess because I hate to clean it. Sometimes I forget and leave wet towels on my bed after I get out of the tub. Sometimes I leave dirty socks on my floor, then they get kicked under the bed. Then my mother gets mad and makes me clean it up. She says I cannot go out of my room until it is clean. I hate to clean it up, but I have to. I can't wait till I'm a grown-up, then I won't have to do anything I don't want to do. That's what I told Mom. Mom said that even grown-ups have to do work and things they don't want to do. Mom said that there will always be times in my life that I have to do things I don't want to do, so I need to start now. I have to ask Jesus to help me face my work. Jesus had to work too, so He understands.

When I think about all these things in this book, I try to ask someone about them. Then I know I can always talk to God about anything. He knows everything about me anyway, and He knows everything about the whole world and everyone in it. Even when I think bad thoughts, and even when I think about doing things that are wrong, I can still tell God. He will not hate me or be mad. He will understand. If I'm having a hard time doing the right things, I can ask God about it, and He will help me. He is so cool.

2

My name is Dustin. I play baseball for the Colorado Rockies at Davis Field. One time, I was in the outfield and the other team was at bat. They hit the ball far, but I finally got it off the ground and ran to third base and touched the guy and got him out. I really did get him out; my dad saw it and so other kids' dads, but the umpire said he was safe, but he was really out. I told the umpire the truth five times, but he would not believe me. My dad told him too, but the umpire would not believe my dad.

I was so mad, I felt like spitting, but I didn't. That was not fair. I know that you can't always act out your anger. Dad said that is self-control. Dad said a lot of times, people treated Jesus very unfairly. Jesus got mad sometimes, but he used self-control.

I have a friend named Corey. One time Corey and I walked to the Circle K store. I bought Sweetarts and Bazooka, but Corey's mother wouldn't give him any money, so do you know what Corey did? He tore the pocket out of the inside of his jacket. Then he stole a Butterfinger candy bar and stuffed it way in the back of his jacket through the hole in that pocket. He said even if he got caught, his pockets would be empty, so no one would know he did that.

He showed me how to do it, but I wouldn't because I know it's wrong to take something that doesn't belong to you, even if you think you won't get caught. I still think that someday, Corey really will get caught. Even if he doesn't get caught by the store worker, he still won't get away with stealing, because you can't hide anything from God. God sees everything, and He knows everything too. Even if Corey's mom never knows he stole, God will know.

I did a science project that I though was really cool. It was a clay volcano that really would erupt. All you had to do was put some vinegar and baking soda inside, and it would bubble up and fiz out. I did it all by myself. My friend Brendon did his project, and he thought it was cooler than mine. He did planets that light up when you push a button. Brendon's dad did this for him, but I did my own work. Brendon won first place. No wonder, a grown-up really did it. That was not fair at all. I told my teacher that, and she said even if I didn't win from the judges, I won in my heart because I did the work myself and could be proud of that. My teacher said sometimes even when you follow all the rules, things don't always turn out fair.

My dad bought me a big bucket full of tongue splasher bubble gum. I kept it on my dresser. One day, all my friends came over to my house. They started to take handfuls of my gum, not just one piece. I told on them. Then I hid my gum. I never want to share anything with them again. Mom said I should try to forgive them and still share with them, one piece at a time. They didn't even say they were sorry. Would you want to share with someone who stole your gum? It is not easy to be nice to other people when they are creepy to you. Mom said that Jesus never asks us to do anything that He didn't do Himself. Jesus understands how hard it is to be nice to mean people. Before men hung Jesus on the cross, they beat Him and slapped Him in the face. They even spit on Him. They whipped Him until He bled and His skin was cut open. He was not mean back. He just asked God, His Father, to forgive them.

It's me again, Dustin Lewis. I play football for a team called the Pinellas Park Thunderbirds. Last fall, a coach from our league lied about the age of one of his players. The league leaders found out about the lie and suspended all of the Thunderbirds players for a whole year. I don't think it's fair for all those kids to be punished for one kid's lie. Mom said that everything we do in our life affects other people. Now I see how one person's lie hurt over four hundred kids. It is so important to be fair. Winning games is fun, but honesty is better.

Here is a dead lizard for my sister's pillow.

My cat killed a lizard. It was fat and brown and ugly. Since my sister is always mean to me, I put that dead lizard on her pillow to try to try to freak her out. My mom said that it was wrong to do that, even though my sister is mean sometimes. My mom said when Jesus was on Earth, He returned goodness for meanness, and people learned about love that way. It is hard to give a kind thing in exchange for a mean thing, but if Jesus could do it, so can I. It might even change my sister's mean ways. I tried it one day. She was making fun of me on the school bus in front of my friends. Instead of fighting with her, I gave her a piece of fudge out of my lunch box. It was hard to do and I didn't really want to, but I did. My sister didn't even say thanks. She just took the fudge, but she did stop making fun of me on the bus.

I went to the state fair, and I won three goldfish. All you had to do was throw a ball in a bowl of water and you got a goldfish. It looked easy, but it was hard. I wasted a lot of money trying to win, but finally I won. My sister cried because she didn't have any fish, so my mom bought her three fish at the pet store. My goldfish lived in my bedroom in a big glass jar. My sister threw a cherry Pop-Tart in my fish bowl and when I came home from school, my fish were dead. She told my mom it was an accident, but I don't think it was. Then I felt like throwing something in her fish bowl, but my dad said not to try to get even with other people. My dad said it is wrong to try to get revenge. My dad said that the Lord is the only one who is supposed to deal with other people's unfair ways, and He is able to make all things fair in the end, even if it is not the way we think He should.

My friend Jimmy doesn't have a dad, he only has a mother. When my dad takes me to spring-training baseball games, I think it makes Jimmy sad. My dad takes me to Chuck E Cheese and McDonald's too. Sometimes we take Jimmy with us. We took Jimmy to church with us too. I think maybe that's why Jimmy hangs out at our house so much, especially Friday when Dad brings home pizza. Jimmy's mom didn't sign him up for football because she said it costs too much money. My dad said he would sign Jimmy up. Dad said that God tells us He will be a father to kids who don't have a father. Dad said God wants to use him to help be like a father to Jimmy. Dad said that when we love God and belong to God, we have to look for ways to serve Him and look for ways to do what God wants us to do. God is love and He always wants us to be like Him and love others.

I caught a turtle in the pond behind my house. It was brown and it had a pointy head. Every time you pick it up or touch it. it tucks its head and legs inside its shell. When I caught it, I put it in my tackle box and brought it home. I wanted to keep it in a bucket in my yard. My dad told me that I had to put it in back in the pond, because if I didn't, it might die. That really made me sad, because I really wanted to keep him for a pet. I told Dad I loved him a lot, and I didn't want to let him go.

Dad told me he would be happier and have a better life if I let him go, so I did. When I put him back in the pond, he swam away real fast. I do think Dad was right. My turtle seemed happier in the pond. Dad said that if you really love something, you will do what is best for it even if it makes you sad. Jesus always did what was best for us, even times when it was hard for Him.

My friend James only has two kids in his family, but we are seven kids in our family. James gets to go a lot of places with his family. They go out to eat a lot, and they go to Disney World and Adventure Island and Epcot every summer. They always go out and eat pancakes for breakfast after church every Sunday. Sometimes I wish my family was small, so I could get to go and do all the things that James gets to do. I told that to James one time, and he told me that he wished he had a big family like me. He said he wished he had brothers and sisters, and that he thought that would be more fun than going out to eat and doing all the other stuff he does. I guess God is good to us in different ways. Mom said we have to find all the good things God does for us and thank Him, even if those things are different than other peoples. Mom said sometimes things aren't always so neat as they seem.

This is why God makes rules for our life. He knows us better than we know ourselves because He made us. He makes rules for our life because He loves us. God's rules always work best. Even when it seems like we could get more things or do better by cheating or lying or stealing, it never works. In the end, it only hurts us, and it hurts other people too. God's rules never make our life harder. They make it better. God said in the Bible that He wants our lives to be good.

He wants us to be happy and do well and have good things. He tells us how to do that in the Bible. Then He sent us His son Jesus to show how. What a neat Father He is.